THE Poet AND THE Beauty

Courtney Asunmaa

ISBN
978-1-957378-22-0 (Paperback)
978-1-957378-21-3 (eBook)

FADE IN:

There once was a POET and a BEAUTY. Together, they met and fell in LOVE. Where they spent every waking moment together. Her name was VIOLET and she wrote POETRY. She looked at life as BEAUTY. She looked for the beauty in all things. One day she met a BEAUTIFUL woman and they would start a beautiful romance. Where they got to learn all about each other and fell deeply in love. Their passion for each other was unending. They were so strong and sparks began to fly and never stopped flying. Their story was that of a great love. Their story was of a true love. Their romance was one of passion and love. Where VIOLET was thirty-five years old and ESMERALDA was twenty-one years old. Where VIOLET and ESMERALDA got lost in all of each other. Where they left a trail wherever they went. A beautiful love story remained unraveling.

The CITY comes into view. Then comes into view an independent bookstore comes into view.

FLASH TO:

1. INT. BOOKSTORE/CAFÉ – DAY

The POET was working at a side job at her BOOKSTORE/CAFE as the MANAGER. She was on a break from writing a new poetry novel and was just strolling around the bookstore and making everything there TIDY. VIOLET moved some of the books aside. She then walked over to the CASHIER, REBBA who was at the front of the book store and turned to her before walking out the BOOKSTORE/CAFE front door.

VIOLET
Hey. Rebba. I'm leaving now today.

REBBA
I'll take care of the bookstore. See you later this week.

VIOLET
Thanks. Same here.

2. EXT. STREET - NIGHT

VIOLET held her head down as she carried her BRIEFCASE with her as she walked down the street. Where many cars and people were moving past her.

CUT TO:

3. EXT. OUTSIDE CAFÉ - NIGHT

She sat down at a table that was outside of a cafe. She started writing poetry in her notebook. She was making a novel full of POEMS. The waitress, CHERRY came over.

CHERRY
The usual? Violet.

VIOLET
Yes. Thanks.

CHERRY
No problem.

VIOLET
Thanks. I just don't like to cook when I am living by myself?

CHERRY
Very understandable.

VIOLET
Just working on this novel full of poems that I'm going to publish.

CHERRY
That's great. I enjoy poetry.

CHERRY left and went back into the RESTAURANT. A girl sitting to her at the next table leaned over and spoke to VIOLET.

ESMERALDA

Excuse me. I couldn't help, but hearing you talk to the waitress. I've seen you here writing before. I am quite interested in what you are writing about. May I sit next to you to have a conversation with you?

VIOLET

Sure. You can sit next to me. I don't have anybody to have dinner with, so why not. Have a seat.

ESMERALDA

Thank you. My name is ESMERALDA.

VIOLET

My name is VIOLET.

ESMERALDA

Nice to meet you.

VIOLET

Nice to meet you too. So, now that you know that I write and am a poet. What do you do?

ESMERALDA

I compose music for an opera.

VIOLET

That is outstanding.

ESMERALDA

I have seen you writing everywhere and it peaked my interest. As I do the same.

VIOLET

Really. You are quite unique. Most people take little time out of themselves to notice anything different.

ESMERALDA

That is odd. As I have always found odd people to be the most interesting. As they have the most to say.

VIOLET

Sometimes, the quiet ones have the most to say. Yet, they keep it to themselves until you talk to them or they open up.

ESMERALDA

That is very true. Well. I am glad we are talking.

VIOLET

It is nice to meet you. I noticed you, however, not for writing, but for your looks. You are very good looking. You are beautiful.

ESMERALDA

Why were you too shy to ask me? You are a poet after all?

VIOLET

You are just beautiful. I figured you were already taken. So, why waste my time. Why not find someone else?

ESMERALDA

That is true.

VIOLET

I want much more to this life. I want everything from life. I want the adventure and the extravagance. I want to experience life to its fullest. Where I get everything from life and more.

ESMERALDA

What do you want out of life?

VIOLET

I want a lover. I want to experience everything and more. To get the fullest from life. To experience life. To go exploring. To have no burdens.

ESMERALDA

Where I can go wherever I want. Whenever I want to. I can just pick up and leave everything around me and everyone. To start new elsewhere.

VIOLET

Where I can live my fullest life and make it meaningful. Certain love is beauty. That is my philosophy on life and my philosophy on love.

ESMERALDA

I believe love is a bit different. Love sometimes is like the wind as that it changes direction or speed.

VIOLET

My philosophy on love is that it can be beautiful. It also can be false. Where it wasn't love. Just infatuation.

ESMERALDA

Unrequited love is awful. Yet, it eventually comes back around. Oh. Maybe, that's what we have here.

VIOLET

Love is a bunch of emotions mixed together. Where you can't stop thinking about the other person. Love is beautiful. When love is real, it is everything. Love is loving another more than yourself. Love is about being selfless. Love is about having a soul. You know what? Why are we talking about this? I just met you.

ESMERALDA

I peeked your interest and you started. And we've started to have an interesting conversation. Besides, I know you have the hots for me. I must be making your libido smile.

VIOLET

And how would you notice that?

ESMERALDA

You are blushing and flushed.

VIOLET

You are too much with what are only presumptions.

ESMERALDA

They maybe presumptions, but I do believe that I see you blushing.

VIOLET

It's hot in here.

ESMERALDA

Sure. Whatever you say.

VIOLET

Well, anyways. Love is about the moments that you get swept up and away into. That is what love is all about.

ESMERALDA

Love is never given. Love is earned. Love is about trust. Love is about having things in common. There is no love with no trust. Love is taking your heart and putting it in someone else's hands and expecting them to not break it.

VIOLET

I have thought I was in love, but they proved me wrong. As I was not in love. What about you?

ESMERALDA

I have never been in love either.

VIOLET

Why fall in love, if another is just going to let you down? Makes no sense. Right?

ESMERALDA

Yes. Never leave yourself open to being vulnerable to another. Never a good idea. Am I in your comfort zone yet?

VIOLET

Yes. You are in my comfort zone right now.

ESMERALDA

Same for me.

VIOLET

I've always thought love is supposed to be grand. The bad sometimes leads to a good.

ESMERALDA

Of course.

VIOLET

Love is a game. A game that sometimes you get hurt and sometimes that you don't.

ESMERALDA

Love can be everything that you wanted or absolutely nothing. Where you can be hurt and turn away from it. Yet, never become who did that to you. Chances are that it wasn't even worth it.

VIOLET

Listen to your heart and go with your heart. As your heart longs for another heart that is just beautiful. If your heart is ugly, then your heart will get another ugly.

ESMERALDA

Everybody has a different vision of beauty.

VIOLET

Yes. Some people also have to wear glasses.

ESMERALDA

When you're working your way from the bottom or the middle to get at the top. Nobody wants to be with you. Then, when you're at the top. It is when they all want to be with you. That to me is so classless. Either you are there in the beginning or don't even bother being there at all.

VIOLET

Of course. Isn't that always so?

ESMERALDA

That is so.

VIOLET

My heart is closed, yet is open to beauty and love. Only to someone who deserves it.

ESMERALDA

Love is complicated.

VIOLET

I know that my love is pure and true. Sometimes, the hardest part is letting go, but you have to do because they don't deserve you. Where you deserve better, then that.

ESMERALDA

Sometimes, you also think you must have been both blind and deaf to have loved that person and to have thought you did.

VIOLET

(laughing) Haha. I needed that laughed. Much needed.

ESMERALDA

No problem. Always a pleasure to provide laughter out of a deep conversation.

VIOLET

Charmed over here.

ESMERALDA

I also. We think similar also.

VIOLET

I find beauty in your voice. It calms my heart. You are kind with words.

ESMERALDA

You warm my heart just a little bit. You just need to open your heart a little bit.

VIOLET

Well. I would say that yours is guarded as well. Where the beauty of it all could be endlessly epic.

ESMERALDA

What is love? Is it in another? Is it what you enjoy doing?

VIOLET

The heart searches for hearts that light everything up. As sometimes, things do not become what you wanted. That type of thing happens. It's called life. And humans.

ESMERALDA

Such is life then.

VIOLET

I also think sometimes that having sex with women I don't love is like cheating on me. That I should only have sex with women that I love.

ESMERALDA

That I would agree with then.

VIOLET

Words are but the best things you can do with your lips. The other thing is kissing.

ESMERALDA

Putting them down on paper is as good as speaking them. I like a woman that knows how to speak and write beautifully.

VIOLET

I also. I believe that you can find a beauty in a deep language.

ESMERALDA

That is very true.

The waitress came over and dropped off both of their meals.

CHERRY

Here are your meals at the same time.

VIOLET

Thanks.

ESMERALDA

Thank you.

The waitress left. The two girls then continued talking.

VIOLET

Sometimes, love is like the wind. It blows everywhere. That of which makes it important.

ESMERALDA

Is love predictable or not?

VIOLET

It depends on how high you can get.

ESMERALDA

What are your hobbies?

VIOLET

Writing, drawing, reading, traveling, yachting, and walking outdoors. What about you?

ESMERALDA

Reading, gym, boating, traveling, and shopping.

VIOLET

Shopping? Really?

ESMERALDA

Yes. Anything and everything. I like antiques.

VIOLET

My favorite is used books, old books, first editions, and those kinds of books. The uniqueness of them is interesting.

ESMERALDA

So, I take it you like bookstores. As well as used bookstores.

VIOLET

Especially, used bookstores. You never know what books you will find there. Used bookstores have a bigger selection of books then new bookstores.

ESMERALDA

New bookstores only sell what's popular with books.

VIOLET

Besides, writing a poetry novel. I also own a bookstore that sells both new and used books.

ESMERALDA

I'll have to stop by it sometime then. Is it called 'Booktopia?'

VIOLET

Yes. It is. Smart choice.

ESMERALDA

Unique name.

VIOLET

Yes. I know.

ESMERALDA

I take it your novel is in there.

VIOLET

Yes. It is. This is my second poetry novel that I am working on.

ESMERALDA

That's good.

VIOLET

What are you working on?

ESMERALDA

I am working on my second opera.

VIOLET

Congratulations!

ESMERALDA

I love what I do. So, it's not a waste of my time.

VIOLET

That is good. I also.

ESMERALDA

All of you is becoming all of me.

VIOLET

That is deep.

ESMERALDA

Do you think that it is too much since we just met?

VIOLET

Maybe. Sometimes, all you get is one chance. It is not scaring me away if that is what you are asking me.

ESMERALDA

What not being young about it?

VIOLET

Exactly.

ESMERALDA

You have true beauty.

VIOLET

You are true beauty.

ESMERALDA

I am glad to be your beauty. If I may call myself that?

VIOLET

Yes. You may call yourself my beauty.

ESMERALDA

What are you doing later this week?

VIOLET

Writing. More work. What about you? Nothing special planned. Unless, you want to meet up.

ESMERALDA

I'm just working. There is nothing special going on. We can meet up. We can meet up for the day.

VIOLET

Sounds great!

ESMERALDA

We will then. I'll put my number in your cell phone and you put your number in my cell phone.

They exchanged CELL PHONES. They, then typed in their phone numbers into each other's cell phone and saved it. They handed each other their cell phone back. They went back to their meal.

VIOLET

Here you go.

ESMERALDA

Thanks. We now have both of our numbers.

VIOLET

We can go for a picnic at the lakes and then go out to dinner and the opera later.

ESMERALDA

Sounds like fun.

VIOLET

It should be an amazing time.

ESMERALDA

Yes. It should.

VIOLET

What do you make of what you waste your time doing every day?

ESMERALDA

I envelop my time with joy or things that gives me pleasure.

VIOLET

I know how to give you pleasure if you know what I mean.

ESMERALDA

Seems you've got a sharp mouth.

VIOLET

And tongue if I might add.

ESMERALDA

I won't object.

VIOLET

And I will adhere to that. Remember I call first dibs on that.

ESMERALDA

You are turning out to be what my heart has been searching for.

VIOLET

You also, beauty.

ESMERALDA

You're becoming everything to me.

VIOLET

You also. I feel oddly very strong towards you.

ESMERALDA

You are great personality to have a deep conversation with.

VIOLET

You also. Your words are deep. Words can sometimes be beauty.

ESMERALDA

Beautiful words have true meaning of beauty.

VIOLET

You are a beauty.

ESMERALDA

Well. Thank you. I am flattered.

VIOLET

You know. Having sex with someone, doesn't mean you love them.

ESMERALDA

Yes. There is sex and making love.

VIOLET

You're right. You can have sex with someone that you don't love. You can also have sex with someone that you love.

ESMERALDA

It really is a waste of time and if you think about it quite intrusive to have sex with someone that you do not love.

VIOLET

I would like to only have sex with women I love. As the rest is a waste.

ESMERALDA

As you have such a beautiful voice. I get lost in it.

VIOLET

You whisper sweet words to me.

ESMERALDA

You are so wonderful to be around. I have never met someone that has been quite like you. You are very interesting.

VIOLET

You also. You are interesting as well. That's why I enjoy talking to you. You have a lot to talk about.

ESMERALDA

Have you ever wanted to meet someone and you had a lot to talk about? That is the way I feel about you.

VIOLET

You filled that void for me. We have a lot to talk about. I have never met someone as beautiful as you. You have a beautiful soul. It warms my heart.

ESMERALDA

You warm my heart also. You have a beautiful heart. I can see it in your eyes.

VIOLET

Your eyes pierce through my heart. It's so beautiful. You are a beauty.

ESMERALDA

My eyes lead to my soul.

VIOLET

I have waited for a while for someone like you. I have been searching for such a beauty like you to love for a while. Someone that can make me smile and tickle my heart.

ESMERALDA

I have been waiting for a while also for you. I have waited for a love such as yours. I have high standards.

VIOLET

Will you let me love you?

ESMERALDA

Yes. I believe that you are the only one that could love me like I need to be loved.

VIOLET

Love.

ESMERALDA

I have never loved another. I have never loved another as I have loved you. And I will never love another. Only you.

VIOLET

We just met. We could see that as love at first sight.

ESMERALDA

It is truly beautiful.

VIOLET

That, I'm amazed about.

ESMERALDA

I also. You have a truly beautiful heart.

VIOLET

You as well.

ESMERALDA

I am quite intrigued with our conversation that we have been having. I have never had one of such.

VIOLET

Me either. I am impressed. It's fun talking with you.

ESMERALDA

That is of such greatness. The effect and greatness of words.

VIOLET

Words should be beautiful.

ESMERALDA

You have a love that is truly great.

VIOLET

I can't wait to wake up next to you and with you in my arms.

ESMERALDA

I can't wait to wake up in your arms either.

VIOLET

I can't wait to kiss your forehead and down your body. Where your supple skin tingles with my every kiss.

ESMERALDA

I can't wait for the warmth of your lips leaving a trail of love down my body.

VIOLET

Your body is mine to have.

ESMERALDA

My body is yours to have. You must cherish it.

VIOLET

I will cherish your beautiful body and soul.

ESMERALDA

As I will do unto you.

VIOLET

Your beautiful voice sounds like a whisper in the wind. Where I'm enchanted.

ESMERALDA

I long for your touch.

VIOLET

My heart's survival is in me holding your heart.

ESMERALDA

You hold my heart. As I hold your heart.

VIOLET

That is of such beauty.

ESMERALDA

Beauty comes from love and passion.

VIOLET

I wish to watch you sleep and get lost in how peaceful and beautiful you sleep.

ESMERALDA

That is so cute.

VIOLET

No. You are cute and adorable.

ESMERALDA

We are weaving a tale of our love or is it too early for that?

VIOLET

Nothing is ever too early. It is always too late. Every great love story has a beginning.

ESMERALDA

That is true. Let's hope that it doesn't have an ending.

VIOLET

My heart yearns for another love that is full of passion and beauty. That of which I feel is your love.

ESMERALDA

That of which I feel is your love also.

VIOLET

Your words had me at the very moment you spoke.

ESMERALDA

You as well.

VIOLET

Every tragedy leads to a love story.

ESMERALDA

Yes. I get what you mean by that.

VIOLET

I do wish and long to wake up next to you. Then, I will start out every day happy.

ESMERALDA

I will start out every day with a smile.

VIOLET

That is so. So, it looks like we will both enjoy waking up next to each other.

ESMERALDA

That is true. Such an amazing wonder.

VIOLET

You are an amazing wonder.

ESMERALDA

You also.

They finished their meal. The waitress brought them more drinks and their receipt.

CHERRY

Here is your receipt and drinks.

VIOLET

Thanks.

CHERRY

No problem. It is always a pleasure having you here. I admire unique people a lot and you are interesting to me.

VIOLET

Thanks. I enjoy the food and service.

CHERRY

That is good.

The waitress took their plates and left. VIOLET put down a $100 bill on the receipt. VIOLET then looked back at ESMERALDA.

VIOLET

I took care of the receipt.

ESMERALDA

Thanks. I should have since I came over here.

VIOLET

It was no problem.

ESMERALDA

Really?

VIOLET

Yeah. Why?

ESMERALDA

I didn't want to inconvenience you.

VIOLET

You didn't.

ESMERALDA

What are you doing later?

VIOLET

Maybe, write a bit in my penthouse and then go to sleep. You?

ESMERALDA

Sleep. As I woke up early.

VIOLET

That is very true.

ESMERALDA

You are such a beautiful person.

VIOLET

You are a beauty.

ESMERALDA

I find you to be very amazing. You are kind and gentle.

VIOLET

You are sweet and beautiful.

ESMERALDA

You are so adorable also.

VIOLET

You are a pleasure to my eyes.

ESMERALDA

Everything is so beautiful within your eyes.

VIOLET

Every part of your heart is absolutely spectacular. Your heart sends off sparks.

ESMERALDA

Your heart sends off sparkles.

VIOLET

Where do you see your future?

ESMERALDA

I see it living in a house with a good career. Where I write many more good pieces. In love. Enjoying my life and everything in it. Traveling with my love. What about you?

VIOLET

I see my future as living in a house. Having some vacation places. Having written many more great masterpieces. Opening a business, also expanding my bookstore now. Having lovers. Traveling with a lover. Maybe, even building a house.

ESMERALDA

We both have similarities in what we want or are going for and that is good. As having things in common makes a relationship last longer.

VIOLET

Do you see a future with me?

ESMERALDA

Yes. I do. I know it is soon, but I believe that we were destined for each other. You for me. Me for you.

VIOLET

I do if I look at it. I see a bright future with you.

ESMERALDA

Our future could include both of us. That would be so beautiful.

VIOLET

I am mesmerized in all of your beautiful love.

ESMERALDA

The future looks bright then for the both of us. So beautiful.

VIOLET

So bright.

ESMERALDA

Love is but a mere wonder for one to explore with their lover.

VIOLET

You know. Love sometimes makes you do stupid things. Like you can't see anything, but only your lover.

ESMERALDA

Yes. Love is sometimes like that.

VIOLET

What do you enjoy doing for fun?

ESMERALDA

Traveling, writing, reading, relaxing, walking, hiking, going outdoors, shopping, and going out to new and interesting places.

VIOLET

Traveling, reading, writing, deep conversations, nature, and yachting.

ESMERALDA

All of those are things that we like to do for fun. I also enjoy amusement parks and carnivals.

VIOLET

Yes. I wish there were more of those.

ESMERALDA

I also.

VIOLET

Anything is fun really. It is how you make it fun.

ESMERALDA

That is brilliant. Yes. You can go on something normal and make it fun just by having a good conversation.

VIOLET

That makes a good conversation very great.

ESMERALDA

Deep conversations are always very good. Where with depth conversations provide thought and mind provoking brilliance. They require you to think. They require you to open up your feelings.

VIOLET

Yes. They do require a lot of your emotions. Emotions do run deep and they do require you to think in deep conversations.

ESMERALDA

That is so true.

VIOLET

The key to happiness is to find what you love, what makes you laugh, and what is fun.

ESMERALDA

Yes. What gives you pleasure will make you happy.

VIOLET

Sometimes, in reading a book or play that can make you happy for a bit. It takes you into another world.

ESMERALDA

You are so true about that. Doing that makes you forget about your life for a bit. You get lost in something else.

VIOLET

That is so.

ESMERALDA

Beauty comes in a smile.

VIOLET

Beauty is in one's eyes and when you gaze at them.

ESMERALDA

I get lost in gazing at your eyes. They are beautiful.

VIOLET

Beauty is a wonder that is meant to be explored.

ESMERALDA

I yearn to explore you and let you explore me.

VIOLET

I see passion in your eyes.

ESMERALDA

I hear passion in your voice.

VIOLET

Sometimes, I think that I am thinking about my future as well as my lover's future. A lot. More than them.

ESMERALDA

That would make you a great catch then.

VIOLET

That would.

ESMERALDA

I think life is about the brilliant moments that sweep us away and that we get lost in.

VIOLET

That is true. There is beauty in every word that you speak of.

ESMERALDA

Have you ever had someone that wanted you that you didn't want?

VIOLET

Yes.

ESMERALDA

I also. What did you do?

VIOLET

Politely declined.

ESMERALDA

I also.

VIOLET

Yes.

ESMERALDA

That is so very true

VIOLET

You are right about that.

ESMERALDA

What is so great about that is that love is so amazing.

VIOLET

Well. It is getting late out. I'll call you tomorrow and we will make the next date.

ESMERALDA

Okay. Pick it and make sure it's exciting.

VIOLET

I will. I am so glad that you came over here to sit next to me.

ESMERALDA

I am also. You are so brilliant, funny, and everything that I have been looking for.

VIOLET

You also.

ESMERALDA

I am glad that we met and have spent this time together.

VIOLET

We had the greatest conversation.

ESMERALDA

I am so happy that we met and talked today.

VIOLET

I am excited for our date and our future.

ESMERALDA

I also. I hope we are a part of each other's futures.

VIOLET

That is so amazing.

ESMERALDA

You are so beautiful.

VIOLET

You are too.

ESMERALDA

Good night.

VIOLET

Goodbye until soon.

VIOLET and ESMERALDA got up out of their seats and exited the restaurant.

CUT TO:

4. EXT. PICNIC AT LAKE - AFTERNOON

VIOLET and ESMERALDA were sitting on a BLANKET underneath a cherry blossom tree and were dining on their lunch. People were walking about near the lake.

ESMERALDA

It is such a nice day outside. I'm glad that you picked this for us to do today.

VIOLET

You look very nice today.

ESMERALDA

Why. Thank you. You don't look so bad yourself.

VIOLET

I actually believe it or not put some effort into my appearance today.

ESMERALDA

I'm impressed.

VIOLET

I might be falling in love.

ESMERALDA

I might be in love.

VIOLET

Oh, but it is so wise to put all of one's emotions or cards on the table?

ESMERALDA

Only if you have the better deck.

VIOLET

The scenery out here at the lake is very beautiful.

ESMERALDA

Yes. It is. I am glad you picked this place. I have never been. I would like to come back.

VIOLET

I am glad to have your company today. For you romance has never died.

ESMERALDA

Why. Thank you. You are very witty you know?

VIOLET

Yes.

ESMERALDA

I am very charmed by you.

VIOLET

Glad to be your good luck charm, then I guess.

ESMERALDA

What do you suppose makes for a good time?

VIOLET

I would say laughter, joy, pleasure, excitement, exploring something new, exploring it by yourself or with a lover, and so on.

ESMERALDA

Yes. New things are always good.

VIOLET

Love makes you come and feel alive sometimes.

ESMERALDA

Where something unreal becomes very real. It is amazing. You feel great.

VIOLET

Love is but in the mere words that escape from one's mouth.

ESMERALDA

Everything that comes out of your poetic are beautiful.

VIOLET

Words are meant to be beautiful.

ESMERALDA

Where beauty does come unleashed from words that are poetic.

VIOLET

Such is the importance in a deep conversation.

ESMERALDA

It is mind thrilling and provoking.

VIOLET

Well. I hope now that I have enlightened your mind that I will have the chance to enlighten your pussy.

ESMERALDA

Someone's moving fast.

VIOLET

I'll move at whatever speed you want. I am highly adaptable.

ESMERALDA

That I am charmed with.

VIOLET

Your words are very witty.

ESMERALDA

I am taken with all of you.

VIOLET

As I am with you.

ESMERALDA

I think life is a lot about the chances that we do take. It is also about the chances that we don't take. As for every path that we do or do not take, there is a result for that choice.

VIOLET

Yes. So glad you took the initiative to approach me the other day. If you didn't then we would not be here today.

ESMERALDA

So. I guess that it was good that I made the choice to come and talk to you.

VIOLET

Yes. It was also good that I made the choice to talk to you.

ESMERALDA

Yes. If you were rude with no cause then I would have been turned off.

VIOLET

Is that so? Precious.

ESMERALDA

Yes. It is.

VIOLET

Well. Then.

ESMERALDA

Of course.

VIOLET

What are your plans in life?

ESMERALDA

I would like to fulfill all of my dreams and goals that I have.

VIOLET

Me also.

ESMERALDA

That would just be perfect.

VIOLET

Me as well. Not only for myself, but perhaps lovers.

ESMERALDA

I would agree with that as well.

VIOLET

Who knows, it could be with each other

ESMERALDA

The chances of that are highly likely.

VIOLET

That would be amazing.

ESMERALDA

I would agree.

VIOLET

What do you enjoy the most?

ESMERALDA

Sometimes, I don't mind taking a book and going out to the park to read.

VIOLET

I enjoy that as well.

ESMERALDA

I also don't mind relaxing and talking by the fireplace.

VIOLET

I would agree with you on that as well.

ESMERALDA

Such is a wonder of life.

VIOLET

Life is only fully lived when you're happy or feel alive.

ESMERALDA

Emotions are a beautiful thing.

VIOLET

Everything about the lover's beauty unfolded amongst them.

ESMERALDA

I haven't been able to sleep in the past couple of days, because I've been thinking about you.

VIOLET

I also. I have been thinking about you a lot as well.

ESMERALDA

I think that we make a beautiful couple.

VIOLET

This is what I have been looking for all of my life.

ESMERALDA

I also.

VIOLET

I couldn't be happier than our time that we are spending together now.

ESMERALDA

For our time has been great together.

VIOLET

It will continue on great together our time.

ESMERALDA

A beautiful time indeed.

VIOLET

I could not be happier, then being with you.

ESMERALDA

Me either.

VIOLET

You know back in the older times. You would think that they would think for ahead of their times. Yet, that was not the case.

ESMERALDA

In order to advance, one must think ahead of their time. Not at or prior to their time. That is where nothing new takes place.

VIOLET

It is important to be a forward thinker. Who thinks ahead of their time?

ESMERALDA

As being a forward thinker is important it means you are in advancing in your thoughts.

VIOLET

Something can be everything. If you allow it.

ESMERALDA

Where the wonders of love can dance and blossom everywhere.

VIOLET

Every part of my heart takes yearns for you. My heart likes yours. It feels a sort of comfort towards your heart. A comfort that is beautiful. Where your love is endlessly passionate. I do find myself getting lost in you. I do find myself getting lost in your beauty.

ESMERALDA

I find myself getting lost in your every beautiful word.

VIOLET

Where I almost feel like we belong together.

ESMERALDA

The beauty is everything that makes something amazing.

VIOLET

Love is but a mere wonder.

ESMERALDA

Love is sometimes timed, yet sometimes is timeless.

VIOLET

I see beauty in things.

ESMERALDA

I see beauty in things too.

VIOLET

You are so nice and kind.

ESMERALDA

You are also. I wasn't expecting it.

VIOLET

Why?

ESMERALDA

I don't know. I just wasn't. It was nice and refreshing that you were.

VIOLET

That is good.

ESMERALDA

What do you think of when you think of beauty?

VIOLET

Love, passion, infatuation, irresistibility, longing, desire, pleasure, insatiable, and a lot of other things.

ESMERALDA

Yes. I agree with you as well. You can find beauty in a lot of things. It just is where you look or if you open your eyes.

VIOLET

My eyes are always open, searching for beauty.

ESMERALDA

Mine also.

VIOLET

I do find you to be quite beautiful.

ESMERALDA

Everything with you is stunning.

VIOLET

I think that you are so amazing and spectacular.

ESMERALDA

You also. I enjoy talking and being with you.

VIOLET

I also.

ESMERALDA

I think that it is very nice outside on the lake. We should do this again.

VIOLET

Are we already planning a future or date with me?

ESMERALDA

That is for you to think about, sweetie.

VIOLET

Oh. I see how this is going. Charming.

ESMERALDA

Very nice.

VIOLET

I'm taken with all of your beauty.

ESMERALDA

That I am.

VIOLET

We are beautiful together.

ESMERALDA

I think we make a great couple. I think everybody will be watching us.

VIOLET

That is so very true.

ESMERALDA

It is.

VIOLET

We could make a great couple.

ESMERALDA

Is that you asking me?

VIOLET

Is that you asking me?

ESMERALDA

We shall find out, soon won't we?

VIOLET

Yes. We will. I have to tell you I am difficult to get in a relationship, but I do see a chance with you.

ESMERALDA

It'll happen without either of us knowing it.

VIOLET

Maybe, it has already happened.

ESMERALDA

Charmed.

VIOLET

As I sure you are.

ESMERALDA

What do you think will become of our lives in the future?

VIOLET

Things that we thought would happen.

ESMERALDA

We will. We are but mere lovers to our soul.

VIOLET

You know some people are heartless though. You better watch out for that. Your heart I can tell is naive.

ESMERALDA

I know. That could be a problem, but I'll be able to see it.

VIOLET

That is so very true.

ESMERALDA

What is a life without nothing that you are passionate about or love?

VIOLET

Life is of whatever you make of it.

ESMERALDA

That is what a life consists of. It is what life becomes.

VIOLET

We are products of what our heart longs for?

ESMERALDA

Such is the tale of a heart.

VIOLET

Why should one's heart long for another if they weren't meant to be together?

ESMERALDA

One's love comes undone.

VIOLET

Does love render one to another? I would think so.

ESMERALDA

I would agree with that.

VIOLET

So, what do you think about tonight?

ESMERALDA

I am excited for tonight. I think it should be fun.

VIOLET

Right now is fun. You are the best of company.

ESMERALDA

We become submerged in something deep. Love is deep. Words or deep. A romance is deep. I am glad you took this time to share it with me.

VIOLET

I am glad to share this with you also.

ESMERALDA

We belong together.

VIOLET

You heart belongs to me.

ESMERALDA

What is enjoyable to you?

VIOLET

My newest thing is spending time with you. There aren't many people out there like you.

ESMERALDA

There are many people out there like you either.

VIOLET

I guess that makes the both of us a rare catch.

ESMERALDA

We are a rare catch.

VIOLET

That is of such a thing.

ESMERALDA

I do get taken with you.

VIOLET

As do I with you.

ESMERALDA and VIOLET finished eating and put away their picnic. They, then just relaxed outside.

ESMERALDA

It is nice. Let's stay out a bit and relax.

VIOLET

No problem. It's nice out and I enjoy talking to you.

ESMERALDA

We do have some deep or interesting conversations.

VIOLET

It is never a dull moment with you.

ESMERALDA

That is great.

VIOLET

I enjoy bowling and golfing a bit. What about you?

ESMERALDA

Yes. Those are okay.

VIOLET

Sometimes, I think I guard my heart. You have to though.

ESMERALDA

Yes. I would agree with you on that. I do as well.

VIOLET

What about love scares you the most?

ESMERALDA

Relying on another lover too much. Not only on yourself.

VIOLET

Wouldn't any other way just be settling? Such as companionship.

ESMERALDA

Yes, but who is one to tell you who to love and not?

VIOLET

Your heart is the only one that will tell you who to love.

ESMERALDA

The heart will know when they are in love with another.

VIOLET

That is so.

ESMERALDA

Sometimes, your whole body tingles.

VIOLET

You just know.

ESMERALDA

Sometimes, your heart will think that they love another but they really don't. I really don't. It fills itself with lust.

VIOLET

Well. My heart isn't tricking me with you right now.

ESMERALDA

Is that so? Neither is mine.

VIOLET

So, it looks as if we are both on the same page.

ESMERALDA

Yes. We both are.

VIOLET

You know we are pretty great together.

ESMERALDA

I am intrigued by you.

VIOLET

I want to get to know more about you.

ESMERALDA

We have a love that is very strong and passionate.

VIOLET

I can make all of your dreams and fantasies come true.

ESMERALDA

As I can do for you.

VIOLET

That is so.

ESMERALDA

We are beautiful together.

VIOLET

Yes. We are.

ESMERALDA

That is so very true.

VIOLET

Well. We've been talking for a while and it is starting to get dark.

ESMERALDA

Yes. Let's go over to where our night date is located at.

VIOLET

Yes. We can actually walk from here to the place. I reserved a skyscraper rooftop for dinner over the city. With a great view of the city lights.

ESMERALDA

Okay.

They both started walking out of the park and into the street. Where they passed many shops and cars along the way in the city.

5. EXT. STREET – DUSK

They walked along the street past shops and cars.

VIOLET

The streets look beautifully lit at night.

ESMERALDA

Yes. They do.

VIOLET

Of course.

ESMERALDA

I will probably enjoy this, won't I?

VIOLET

I set it all up for tonight. You'll enjoy dinner.

ESMERALDA

It shall be nice. I am sure.

VIOLET

It shall be very romantic.

ESMERALDA

That is great.

VIOLET

I am quite very thrilled to see you.

ESMERALDA

Yes. You are.

VIOLET

My time with you has been really great.

ESMERALDA

That is so.

VIOLET

That is so very great.

ESMERALDA

I do think that you are the most fun.

VIOLET

I enjoy all of our time that we spend together.

ESMERALDA

I would rather be with no one else.

VIOLET

You are too much. As we have much to talk about.

ESMERALDA

We get taken with all of each other.

VIOLET

Yes.

ESMERALDA

The city is pretty busy today.

VIOLET

Yes. It is.

ESMERALDA

It is very nice.

VIOLET

Yes.

ESMERALDA

We are great together.

VIOLET

I am beginning to think that we should hang out much more together.

ESMERALDA

Same here. I would like that very much.

VIOLET

Me too.

ESMERALDA

We seem to be having almost too much fun and good conversations. That is important.

VIOLET

We are here. Let's go in.

ESMERALDA

Okay.

CUT TO:

6. INT. SKYSCRAPER ROOFTOP - NIGHT

They all went out onto the rooftop. There were ROSE PETALS everywhere. There were lanterns and candles everywhere. There were rose bushes that surrounded them. There meal was out and they sat down and began dinner. It was dimly lit.

VIOLET
I tried.

ESMERALDA
It is beautiful outside here.

VIOLET
So, I guess that I did good.

ESMERALDA
You did well.

VIOLET
You are a beauty.

ESMERALDA
You are so great to me.

VIOLET
Same here

ESMERALDA
You are quite amazing to me.

VIOLET
We belong together.

ESMERALDA
You know that we should really think about moving in together.

VIOLET

Don't you think that it is a little too early for that.

ESMERALDA

Not if I see my future with you and I do.

VIOLET

We have years ahead of us.

ESMERALDA

I don't see my future or living with anybody else. Don't get me wrong. I thought about it. I don't want to be that girl that is like what if and that regrets not getting to live and share my life with you. I don't see myself with anybody else.

VIOLET

I know.

ESMERALDA

I just don't see myself with anybody else right now. You gave me your heart and I am trying to love you the way that you want to be loved. If you would only let me love you. Why can't you trust me? Have I done anything that has made me untrustworthy? No.

VIOLET

No. Not yet.

ESMERALDA

We all have prior experiences that have given us reasons not to trust. It doesn't mean I am like them. I am not.

VIOLET

I know. Blaming you on what someone else has done. That wouldn't be fair to you.

ESMERALDA

That is so.

VIOLET

I know.

ESMERALDA

That is such.

VIOLET

Together, we could fall in love and get lost in the wonders of our love.

ESMERALDA

I like going on dates with you. It's not like it's boring or it feels like a chore or work.

VIOLET

I enjoy dates with you.

ESMERALDA

I enjoy our conversations. They aren't either boring or dull.

VIOLET

I would agree with that.

ESMERALDA

It is not like we are in misery when we are with each other like some people.

VIOLET

That is so.

ESMERALDA

We do belong together in our love.

VIOLET

Our time that we spend together is beautiful.

ESMERALDA

It is.

VIOLET

We are good together.

ESMERALDA

So, what I am saying is that we should think about moving in together soon.

VIOLET

I know. It is just a big deal. I want to live with a girl that gets me and loves me. It is a bit early. I'll think about it.

ESMERALDA

We should. What is the worst that can happen? Nothing.

VIOLET

You could be messy. You could make the bathroom stinky.

ESMERALDA

Very funny. Now, what could be the best?

VIOLET

You could walk around naked or in lingerie. I can get back massages. I can get pampered by you. You can cook.

ESMERALDA

Now, that is where you are wrong. I was thinking that you are pussy whipped. So, you can cook. You can pamper me all the time.

VIOLET

Just because I am a lesbian does not mean I am a cook or like to cook.

ESMERALDA

I was thinking I could sit on the chair and relax and make you bring me water and give me foot massages whenever I wanted.

VIOLET

Hopefully, you're kidding.

ESMERALDA

Not if you want sex. You'll do it.

VIOLET

You are funny.

ESMERALDA

I am not being funny. I am merely saying that if you want to taste my candy. You're going to have go a little beyond that.

VIOLET

Okay. We'll just see how well you can behave yourself. That is when we can decide when to move in together.

ESMERALDA

Do you have any bad habits that I should know about?

VIOLET

I am a bit messy, but I can contain it to my office if I am living with someone. It's mainly my work and paper work stuff. What about you?

ESMERALDA

Nothing.

VIOLET

Oh. Come on, you should have something?

ESMERALDA

I sing a lot. I leave lots of clothes everywhere. I also take a couple of hours to get ready and not a half an hour.

VIOLET

I take a half an hour to get ready.

ESMERALDA

Those aren't anything that is that bad.

VIOLET

Okay.

ESMERALDA

I mean what else could there be there.

VIOLET

Nothing. I guess it is something you find out when you live together.

ESMERALDA

You know that we would have a lot of fun if we lived together.

VIOLET

It would be endlessly fun.

ESMERALDA

Yes. Yes, it would.

VIOLET

We would have so much fun.

ESMERALDA

We could spend hours together and never get bored of each other.

VIOLET

Yes. I agree we probably would never get bored of each other.

ESMERALDA

Yes.

VIOLET

You are a clever one.

ESMERALDA

That you are.

VIOLET

What else would you like?

ESMERALDA

What do you mean?

VIOLET

I mean is there anything else you would like from me?

ESMERALDA

Not that I can think of right now.

VIOLET

Picky.

ESMERALDA

No. It just means that I have high standards.

VIOLET

Well. Props to you for having high standards.

ESMERALDA

As I am sure you do. Maybe, that's why we fit well together.

VIOLET

That is so beautiful. High standards are always good.

ESMERALDA

You amaze me. Such a great humor.

VIOLET

A good humor has always just come to me naturally.

ESMERALDA

That is so.

VIOLET

Yes.

ESMERALDA

What do you make of this all?

VIOLET

Of what?

ESMERALDA

Of it all?

VIOLET

If you mean us and the path that we are going down. Then, I say that we are doing very well indeed.

ESMERALDA

I would agree also. I think we have a very good future ahead of us.

VIOLET

As we do have a future together.

ESMERALDA

Probably, because we get along so well. As we know what each other thinks.

VIOLET

That is so.

ESMERALDA

We do.

VIOLET

I know.

ESMERALDA

It is so beautiful out. The view is great.

VIOLET

Yes. I have always enjoyed a view of the city lights.

ESMERALDA

I do also.

VIOLET

Do you plan on doing anything interesting this week?

ESMERALDA

I don't know yet. You?

VIOLET

Probably working in my bookstore for a bit. Just checking up on it.

ESMERALDA

Sounds like a plan. Getting work done. That's always a positive.

VIOLET

Everything belongs together beautifully you know that.

ESMERALDA

We fit together beautifully.

VIOLET

It is such a nice night out.

ESMERALDA

Yes. It is.

VIOLET

Indeed.

ESMERALDA

What do you think would be a fun thing to do while traveling?

VIOLET

I have always enjoyed the mountains, the beach, the jungle, and other things. What about you?

ESMERALDA

I enjoy the beach, caves, tropics, and other stuff as well.

VIOLET

I like going on fun adventures.

ESMERALDA

Me also.

VIOLET

That is what makes life so fun and lively.

ESMERALDA

I like adventures also. I am an explorer.

VIOLET

Anything that is exciting, then I am game for.

ESMERALDA

I like getting thrills or the adrenaline rush, but not too much.

VIOLET

I would agree with you as well.

ESMERALDA

That is so.

VIOLET

You know I do believe that you still owe me a kiss or so.

ESMERALDA

Don't push your luck.

VIOLET

You know you love me as I am adorable.

ESMERALDA

That is so very true.

VIOLET

Such a feisty beauty and I love it.

ESMERALDA

You are quite something.

VIOLET

That indeed. As you are too.

ESMERALDA

Charmed to say the least.

VIOLET

It was all my pleasure in charming you.

ESMERALDA

It is all too much.

VIOLET

Yes. So, what are your passions?

ESMERALDA

My passions are in things that I enjoy doing or opera.

VIOLET

Mine is poetry or reading. Other such things.

ESMERALDA

Well. I think we are also both getting to be passionate about each other. That's good.

VIOLET

We are both passionate about each other. So that is very good.

ESMERALDA

You are so beautiful.

VIOLET

Everything is so great. You know we are having a great day so far. I am glad we had another date.

ESMERALDA

I am also.

VIOLET

You are truly funny.

ESMERALDA

You are funny as well.

VIOLET

You surrender yourself to me. You're hot, sexy and loving.

ESMERALDA

Really nice.

VIOLET

Would you think it was funny if I put the diamond ring in your pussy and you had to get it out?

ESMERALDA

It better be a good one.

VIOLET

See. I knew it.

ESMERALDA

If the depth of your heart glistens throughout everything. Then, beauty emerges.

VIOLET

To know is to be informed.

ESMERALDA

If I was a fire alarm inspector. Then, I would inspect the fire in your pants.

VIOLET

You could bring the fire extinguisher.

ESMERALDA

Are you going to the party tonight?

VIOLET

What party?

ESMERALDA

The party in my pants.

VIOLET

Really nice.

ESMERALDA

It is so romantic out here.

VIOLET

Yes. It is.

ESMERALDA

If you know what I mean. You have to stop dipping your hands in all of the cookies jar. I know there are many delicious flavors.

VIOLET

I know, but there are so many flavors and they are tasty. I just want a lot of them.

ESMERALDA

We can't always have what we want.

VIOLET

It's like being in a candy store. Where you want to eat all of the delicious candy.

ESMERALDA

I have candy for you, VIOLET. If you behave yourself.

VIOLET

Oh. Do you now?

ESMERALDA

Yes. I do and it's very tasty.

VIOLET

I am interested. You may continue.

ESMERALDA

Love is but a mere game to explore.

VIOLET

Love is but a game that I enjoy winning on.

ESMERALDA

Well. Of course. Nobody likes to lose.

VIOLET

That is how it goes.

ESMERALDA

Quite thrilled over here at the moment if you can tell.

VIOLET

I can.

ESMERALDA

I can see I nabbed a jewel being, you.

VIOLET

My love is like a diamond. Priceless.

ESMERALDA

Your love is priceless.

VIOLET

Touching.

ESMERALDA

Our conversations are always deeply moving and touching.

VIOLET

That is so. I have begun to notice the patterns.

ESMERALDA

We are just in the process of exploring and learning about each other. From our hearts to everything else.

VIOLET

I am having fun being VIOLET, the explorer.

ESMERALDA

That you are.

VIOLET reaches over and places her hand over ESMERALDA's hand on the table.

VIOLET

Do you feel that? I can make your body tingle. Where sparks fly off in your heart. If you feel something, you feel everything.

ESMERALDA

Your touch is soft and gentle.

VIOLET

I feel passion in this touch. A derived a pleasure is what I am experiencing.

ESMERALDA

If I didn't know better, then I would think that you are trying to seduce me.

VIOLET

And if I didn't know any better, then I would say it was working.

ESMERALDA

Charmed. You are very clever, but I can see that. Maybe, you are charming, but one has to also let herself be charmed. Otherwise, it won't happen.

VIOLET

Ah, but what is a love without the seduction?

ESMERALDA

And what lack the excitement and spontaneity? I think not.

VIOLET then took her off of ESMERALDA. They went back to their meal. Pausing to talk in between eating dinner.

VIOLET

I in return would also like to be seduced.

ESMERALDA

Relationships are all about spontaneity. They actually fail without it.

VIOLET

The lack thereof makes a relationship flop.

ESMERALDA

A relationship needs to sizzle with everything. You need a lot of emotions to keep it going.

VIOLET

That is so.

ESMERALDA

So, what are the pros and cons of being in a relationship.

VIOLET

I'm going to take your virtue. I'm going to take something special from you. Your heart will be mine.

ESMERALDA

Is that so? So, I will lose my virtue. I would think I would be virtuous.

VIOLET

That is very true per say.

ESMERALDA

What do you think about being wooed or seduced?

VIOLET

If it comes from the right person, then I would say that I love it.

ESMERALDA

There are however, not honest and sneaky people out there.

VIOLET

I know. That's why it is fun to be done to as well as doing.

ESMERALDA

Ah. Lovely.

VIOLET

Seduction is brilliant. It is almost like a game and how well that you can play it.

ESMERALDA

The better you play it; the more the other is infatuated with you.

VIOLET

That is so.

ESMERALDA

You are beautiful with words.

VIOLET

Courting goes the same way. As it's going on a bunch of romantic dates.

ESMERALDA

I enjoy being courted then. As I like being taken on romantic dates.

VIOLET

That also depends on the person.

ESMERALDA

That is so.

VIOLET

I get lost in all of who you are as a person.

ESMERALDA

You are the soul that sings out to me.

VIOLET

You are everything that I have always wanted and more.

ESMERALDA

You are everything that I have always wanted and more.

VIOLET

As we keep learning more about each other.

ESMERALDA

We keep growing into each other. We keep growing together.

VIOLET

We keep getting higher together.

ESMERALDA

I fall in love with you every day.

VIOLET

I fall in love with you even more everyday also.

ESMERALDA

You are so romantic and that is part of what I like about you.

VIOLET

There is such a beautiful moment in everything we do together.

ESMERALDA

Yes. There is.

VIOLET

We are writing our love story. Do you know that?

ESMERALDA

Yes. I do. It is turning out to be quite beautiful.

VIOLET

Yes. It is beautiful.

ESMERALDA

What would a love story be without you?

VIOLET

What would a love story be without a beauty?

ESMERALDA

Have you ever been cheated on?

VIOLET

Depends on what you consider to be cheating?

ESMERALDA

Just cheating. Where someone else has sex with another.

VIOLET

It is cheating yourself, because you could be having me.

ESMERALDA

Yeah. I would agree some people are so heartless when they cheat. Especially, when they cheat with other heartless people.

VIOLET

Whatever, though they don't know it. They got nothing and everything they didn't want. Their misfortune is your fortune.

ESMERALDA

You must be hiding a lot of pain in that quietness.

They both stopped eating. They looked at each other and talked while being serious.

VIOLET

Pain just makes you feel alive and not numb.

ESMERALDA

Numb is just a feeling of apathy.

VIOLET

Whatever in the end you know that you leave the cheating person. As you lost your trust in them and they hurt you. That is a betrayal and its hurts so bad. That tears weep down my cheeks. Where then pain is so unbearable that it stings unbearably. It's like your screaming in your head and nobody else can see. You're a facade and nobody else can see it, but you. Essentially.

ESMERALDA

That is very cruel. Indeed. It's people. Oh well. Sometimes, people don't know what they have until it's gone.

VIOLET

I would like to think that.

ESMERALDA

You learn to move on from heartbreak. It's inevitable.

VIOLET

Moving on from heartbreak is like saying I hope it doesn't happen again. When can I do better or differently?

ESMERALDA

Will you love like you have never been hurt?

VIOLET

Yes. I can love like I have never been hurt.

ESMERALDA

Will you ever look back on those you used to love or would you move on?

VIOLET

I'll never look back. They made it easy not to look back by being heartless and cheating.

ESMERALDA

Having your heart just means maybe you should have done things differently or faster. It is just the way that it is. Maybe, it wasn't meant to be. Maybe, there is no destiny. Maybe, the heart searches for another in vain.

VIOLET

Heartbreak is not fun. You see your whole world and what you thought was your future falling apart. Your heart gets crushed. You feel it falling apart and there is nothing you can do to stop it. It sheds tears that flood you. All you want to do is escape to someplace else that is happy.

ESMERALDA

The heartbreak can lead to pain. At least you now know what you don't want in the future.

VIOLET

Heartbreak hurts, because you see that they moved on with another. Even if they can't see that lie that they are living. You'll move on from heartbreak. You just have to tell your next girlfriend that.

ESMERALDA

Well. You should be telling me. I would think your next girlfriend should know if any girls had actually, hurt your heart. That you actually loved or maybe thought that you loved. It is one thing to think that you have loved someone without ever having met and been with them. Then, to have really loved them and have been with them and spoken to them. Those are two different things. Love is a bit like that.

VIOLET

What about love at first sight? What about love at first read? It just isn't there. Love at first read, yes.

ESMERALDA

You can't just lie to your next girlfriend and be like no I didn't accidentally love the wrong girls. You need to tell them that your heart was broken and that your moving on and not looking back.

VIOLET

Maybe, I've never really been in love, because they won't have cheated and left me. I guess that it is better than sooner or later. As they would leave me anyways. Better to do it sooner rather than later. Even if your life arrives late to the party.

ESMERALDA

Such is the pain of heartbreak. You know that I might just be the girl to put your heart back together.

VIOLET

Heartbreak is not pleasant. It hurts and is very painful. As you thought that you loved someone with all of your heart and it was stolen away from you. That is just what happens.

ESMERALDA

What if the heart is breakable?

VIOLET

Only in love.

ESMERALDA

Does your heartbreak affect me?

VIOLET

What is a heart meant for if it isn't meant to be broken?

ESMERALDA

Such is heartbreak.

VIOLET

Having your heart broken. It is like feeling your heart break into pieces and you can't do anything about. The tears fall around you. It is everything, yet nothing.

ESMERALDA

Sometimes, I wish that you would look at me the way you looked at her. I know that might never happen, but it could because we have met. I want you to look at me the way you look at those girls or other girls. I want that. I don't know if I'll ever get that.

VIOLET

Yeah, but if you're going to look at girls like that then they better look like that. Otherwise, they are a facade and fake. It wasn't love. It's just a delusion. Where you tried to fit and make someone into something that they are not.

ESMERALDA

Either way sometimes. Sometimes things fall apart and everything crumbles. It's called life. Life isn't bright. Look at us we are already fighting and arguing about this.

VIOLET

No. You can't argue about something that isn't there.

ESMERALDA

What? So, you're saying that I can see someone that is there, but not there? That I see someone, but they are so far gone at this point. I can just sit here and look at you and see this.

VIOLET

One is never so far gone at a point. It is only in stupidity, ignorance, and being heartless that you can't see it. Like I said, some people have a soul and others don't.

ESMERALDA

What about if I see everything and I want to stay and not leave. I see in beauty in this. What if I won't leave you?

VIOLET

You are only saying it for the present and not the future. I don't have time for something and not everything.

ESMERALDA

Such is life. Fucking peachy. Is this how I should take it?

VIOLET

No. You should get a beer. Then, you should you be what I want. Figure it out.

ESMERALDA

Oh. Really how about I dump the beer on you?

VIOLET

What no champagne?

ESMERALDA

You are such a little twat.

VIOLET

I'm your annoyance though. Don't worry. I'll mark that vagina as mine. Probably. If you're not going to hit my vagina and heart.

ESMERALDA

You know if you never let anyone in. You'll always be alone.

VIOLET

No. I have my writings. Even amongst the rewrites and heartless women. Don't you forget that.

ESMERALDA

Fine. You can sit there in dwell in them and let them consume them or open your heart to me.

VIOLET

What looking to fix a broken heart? Isn't that a bit of rubbish.

ESMERALDA

What. You want to be another notch on the wall. I'm not like that.

VIOLET

They all say that.

ESMERALDA

Well. I mean it.

VIOLET

Heartbreak is painful, but you either move on or don't. Then, you find girls that won't break your heart.

ESMERALDA

What? You have never broken a girl's heart? You are a liar.

VIOLET

No. I never have broken a girl's heart. Thank you very much.

ESMERALDA

Isn't that just a coincidence?

VIOLET

Heartbreak isn't fun. You'll get over it though eventually. Time moves on. People move on. Wake up from your dreams and see reality. It's there. You just can't see it.

ESMERALDA

(angry) I see. I don't know who you want me to be. I can't be those girls. Nor can I pretend to be. You want me to become better. I can't deal with your shit.

VIOLET

(angry) Fine. Go fuck another loser and heartless asshole. I don't fucking care anymore. Do you get that?

ESMERALDA

(angry) Fuck you!

VIOLET

(angry) Yeah! I didn't fuck you, yet. You know though in truth you already fucked yourself and I didn't have to do anything. I hope I eventually learn to love someone. Maybe, you.

ESMERALDA

Oh great.

VIOLET

What if you had a way to truthfully look at girls. Yes. Okay.

ESMERALDA

Heartbreak isn't fun. That is just how it is.

VIOLET

No. It isn't. I'm getting over it though. You are helping as well.

ESMERALDA

That is good. Move on.

VIOLET

I'm channeling my inner happiness. And it's coming from my pants.

ESMERALDA

Real charming. At least you can still make yourself laugh. You look pretty when you smile.

VIOLET

Love is but a mere heart of passion. We are but two hearts dancing together.

ESMERALDA

We were both destined for greatness.

VIOLET

We should be great together. It will be better that way.

ESMERALDA

You are a dream come true.

VIOLET

You are also.

ESMERALDA

Life is but a journey of one's heart.

VIOLET

Yes. Filled with different choices and paths.

ESMERALDA

Well. It's getting late.

VIOLET

I know. My place is a penthouse in this building if you want to go back to it and spend the night.

ESMERALDA

It would be a pleasure.

VIOLET

Let's get going.

ESMERALDA

Sure.

VIOLET

Let's go.

CUT TO:

7. INT. PENTHOUSE - NIGHT

VIOLET and ESMERALDA passionately started kissing as they made their way into VIOLET's penthouse. VIOLET kissed ESMERALDA and then started fumbling with the kisses to the front door as she opened the door to her penthouse. VIOLET then turned around and locked the front door. Then, they start to kiss again. VIOLET's back was against the door. Then, VIOLET grabbed ESMERALDA's hand and lead her into her master bedroom. Where they took off their clothes down to their lingerie and climbed into bed. They were passionately kissing for a bit.

VIOLET

Your kiss makes my whole body tingle with passion.

ESMERALDA

Your kiss lingers on my lips.

VIOLET

I get lost in your kiss.

ESMERALDA

Your kiss makes me feel alive.

VIOLET

Your kiss makes all of my emotions come undone.

ESMERALDA

Your body is so soft.

VIOLET

Your body is beautiful.

ESMERALDA

Hold me as we fall asleep.

VIOLET

We'll spoon.

VIOLET spooned ESMERALDA from behind. VIOLET pulled the bed covers over them. They closed their eyes and went to sleep.

ESMERALDA

Good night.

VIOLET

Night, sweetie.

CUT TO:

8. INT. PENTHOUSE - MORNING

They were in their bikini's. They went and grabbed two flyboards. They, then walked outside of their penthouse onto the beach.

FLASH TO:

9. EXT. BEACH - AFTERNOON

They were in the ocean and using their fly boards. Where they were zipping along over the ocean.

VIOLET

(shouting) This is so much fun!

ESMERALDA

(shouting) Yes. This is fun! Good idea!

They continued flyboarding over the ocean and having fun. They were laughing and enjoying themselves. Eventually, they finished and they took their flyboards off. They, then swam back to the shore and put their flyboards down next to their blankets that they had laid out on the beach. They, then laid out in their bikinis on the beach. Where they relaxed for a bit.

VIOLET

Well. That was fun.

ESMERALDA

Yes. That was very fun.

VIOLET

That is so.

ESMERALDA

Good choice for fun things to do. Flyboarding is very fun.

VIOLET

Thought you would enjoy it.

ESMERALDA

This is relaxing. Nothing like having time off from work to relax and enjoy your life.

VIOLET

Work really hard and sacrifice time. Then, later you can go off and have fun doing whatever that you want.

ESMERALDA

If you sacrifice some of your time now. Then, later you can go out and have more fun.

VIOLET

As a sacrifice that you have now is going to leave you with more time later.

ESMERALDA

That is so.

VIOLET

So, we are enjoying that now. Where we are getting to relax now.

ESMERALDA

It is so hot out here.

VIOLET

Yes. It is in two ways.

ESMERALDA

Nice one.

VIOLET

Glad to make you smile.

ESMERALDA

That is great that you live on the beach. I live in the city.

VIOLET then leaned over and lay between ESMERALDA's legs. VIOLET stoked the sides of her legs. Then, VIOLET kissed her lips.

VIOLET

Your lips taste very supple and your skin is so smooth.

ESMERALDA

My body is tingling.

VIOLET

You are so beautiful. You know that?

ESMERALDA

Thank you.

VIOLET

Well. I am going to keep telling you that.

ESMERALDA

You know I can't stop thinking about. When I am not doing anything. I just start to think about you.

VIOLET

Oh. Really?

ESMERALDA

Yes.

VIOLET

I have got a confession to make. I think about you all of the time.

ESMERALDA

Well. It looks like we both do. So, we got that going for us. Now, don't we?

VIOLET

Yes, we do.

ESMERALDA

My heart is beating faster for you. Place your hand on it.

ESMERALDA took VIOLET's hand and placed it on her heart.

VIOLET

I feel your beating heart. It is beautiful.

ESMERALDA

You have captured my heart.

VIOLET

Your body is so soft and supple.

VIOLET then took her hand off of ESMERALDA's heart and then rolled back over onto her blanket. Where they were both relaxing.

ESMERALDA

I am becoming quite smitten with you.

VIOLET

Oh really? Didn't you say that you weren't seduced or impressed by my charm?

ESMERALDA

No. I just said that it would be hard and it would have to be true love.

VIOLET

Well. I am mighty impressed with you so far.

ESMERALDA

You mean that I have yet to fuck it up?

VIOLET

I guess that would mean that I would have yet to fuck it up too?

ESMERALDA

I guess so.

VIOLET

I am quite romantic or at least try to be when in love and infatuated with someone.

ESMERALDA

I like romance as it gives you something unique to experience.

VIOLET

Especially, when another is insatiable.

ESMERALDA

Is that so?

VIOLET

Yes. It is so.

ESMERALDA

The idea of you is absolutely quite ravishing too be honest.

VIOLET

Just as you are to me.

ESMERALDA

You are very charming and clever. That is to say the least.

VIOLET

When think about the future in twenty years from now. Do you see me with you or do you someone else with you?

ESMERALDA

Depends. We are doing very well now and we just got started a little bit ago. Yes. I know some might say that it's too early to judge that, but I do see a future with you. And, I don't see a future with anybody else.

VIOLET

I see my future with you. Perhaps. I'm mostly likely in tuned to thinking.

ESMERALDA

I'm in tuned to your emotions.

VIOLET

Your love has the deepest of depths. As does mine for you.

ESMERALDA

I quite enjoy my time that I spend with you. It is a pleasure.

VIOLET

I enjoy my time spent with you as well. You are a pleasure as well.

ESMERALDA

We have some great and interesting conversations.

VIOLET

I like how we can talk about anything and everything. I like how we can have deep conversations that go on forever.

ESMERALDA

I just like getting lost in your voice and words.

VIOLET

Your beauty will forever dazzle before me.

ESMERALDA

That is true to its utmost form.

VIOLET

If you think about it. The language words can actually be used quite poetically and beautifully.

ESMERALDA

Where the words that are spoken from one's lips can console another. Where you hear of beauty.

VIOLET

Yes. That is why words sometimes are so important.

ESMERALDA

It is starting to get late out. Let's go in and shower and then get ready for tonight.

VIOLET

Okay.

They gathered their blankets and flyboards and then went back into VIOLET's penthouse

CUT TO:

10. INT. VIOLET'S BOOKSTORE/CAFÉ - NIGHT

VIOLET and ESMERALDA were seated at one of the tables. VIOLET had dimly lit the room and there were candles that surrounded them. They were eating the dinner there that VIOLET had prepared for them. VIOLET Dinner is served.

ESMERALDA

Thank you.

VIOLET

I picked my bookstore and cafe to bring you to tonight for dinner, because I thought that you might like to see it.

ESMERALDA

Of course. It is splendid.

VIOLET

It is a large collection. So, there are a lot of new and used books from a variety of different novels.

ESMERALDA

Excellent. I always have loved a good read.

VIOLET

Me too.

ESMERALDA

Very romantic.

VIOLET

You like romance.

ESMERALDA

Depending upon the individual, but yes.

VIOLET

Romance always brightens a relationship up.

ESMERALDA

That is true.

VIOLET

Dinner is edible.

ESMERALDA

Real nice. Good job. You didn't burn the food. Very impressed.

VIOLET

I try. What can I say?

ESMERALDA

So, what made you open the bookstore and cafe?

VIOLET

My novel and that it needed to be marketed in such a way. I also thought that it would be neat somewhere along the line to open my own bookstore and cafe.

ESMERALDA

Good for you. That's great.

VIOLET

It's even better because I got to make you dinner and we can now eat here. Makes a different change from the restaurant.

ESMERALDA

That is true. It is different from a restaurant.

VIOLET

I noticed your beautiful cleavage has come out tonight to play. It's like another set of eyes for me to stare at.

ESMERALDA

Oh, so piercing. Really nice, VIOLET.

VIOLET

It is better to be attracted to one's goodies. Think of them as your bait to lure me. Then, you'll eventually catch me. At least I am not distracted by other less pleasurable sights. Nor should one be nonchalant about it. What beautiful wonders your cleavage presents. Your cleavage gives me pleasure.

ESMERALDA

Is that so?

VIOLET

It's like the candy mountains splurged out in for the scenic view. Quite the delightful sight.

ESMERALDA

I can see your breasts as well.

VIOLET

I know that. Charming.

ESMERALDA

Is that so?

VIOLET

Yes.

ESMERALDA

Clever one.

VIOLET

Time is on our side right now.

ESMERALDA

What if time was meant to be bent and we were meant to be time.

VIOLET

Everything about you my love is beautiful.

ESMERALDA

Aww.

VIOLET

There I go to seek your wonderful breasts of pleasure. I'm an explorer of your body.

ESMERALDA

You're meant to get lost from within pleasuring my body. So, don't think that you will be going anywhere anytime soon. I indeed plan to take advantage of this. You will satisfy my sexual cravings and much more.

VIOLET

Hmm. Is that so? Are you asking or telling me that?

ESMERALDA

That is for me to decide and for you to question.

VIOLET

What if I want to satisfy your sexual cravings?

ESMERALDA

Then, we shall be fulfilled with much pleasure.

VIOLET

Yes. Indeed.

ESMERALDA

I am so enlightened by your love.

VIOLET

Is that so? Yes. It is so.

ESMERALDA

That is but a mere mention of how my heart longs for you.

VIOLET

It is what it is. That is that.

ESMERALDA

Such is the journey that one must take in love should they chose that path.

VIOLET

Love has many different paths that you can take. The most fun are the ones that give you the most pleasure. That makes you laugh and smile. They are the ones that dance from within a romance. They make you feel all of your emotions. They make you feel alive.

ESMERALDA

You make me feel all of those. So, I take it that I have gone down many different paths of our love.

VIOLET

Our love is blossoming beautifully.

ESMERALDA

I am so excited for you and your bookstore and cafe. Also, for your previous poetry novel and upcoming poetry novel.

VIOLET

I'm glad that you are thrilled. Before we leave you can grab a couple of books to take with you. It's on me. As well as mine of course.

ESMERALDA

Thanks. No problem. I'm thrilled with you. That is great.

VIOLET

I'm glad that you like it.

ESMERALDA

Our time together has been absolutely great.

VIOLET

Yes. I would agree. Our time has been wonderful. I feel myself falling in love with you every day. It's as though we were meant to be together.

ESMERALDA

We do belong together that I must say here.

VIOLET

You are so beautiful to me. I can just get hypnotized by starring at your beauty. To me you are beauty.

ESMERALDA

You aren't so bad yourself.

VIOLET

Beauty is absolutely amazing.

ESMERALDA

Dinner was good. Thanks.

VIOLET

You're welcome. Go ahead and go pick some books while I put the dishes in the kitchen.

ESMERALDA

Okay. Thanks.

11. INT.BOOKSTORE - NIGHT

ESMERALDA left and strolled through the bookstore and started looking through the book selection.

12. INT. CAFÉ KITCHEN - NIGHT

VIOLET put the dishes in the kitchen sink and left and joined ESMERALDA.

13. INT.BOOKSTORE - NIGHT

VIOLET walked up to ESMERALDA and hugged her and held her from behind. ESMERALDA was pulling books in and out of the shelves and had five in her hands.

VIOLET

Hello. Gorgeous.

ESMERALDA

Hey. I got five books. I am ready to go.

VIOLET

That was quick.

ESMERALDA

I had planned on visiting the bookstore sometime soon. I just hadn't had the time lately.

VIOLET

Let's get going sweet lips. I need some sweet loving tonight.

ESMERALDA

Oh. Naughty. I love it.

VIOLET

Let's go.

FLASH TO:

14. INT. VIOLET'S PENTHOUSE BEDROOM - NIGHT

VIOLET and ESMERALDA were walking along the beach together and holding hands. ESMERALDA then jumped on VIOLET's back and rode her back. They both laughed. VIOLET then put ESMERALDA down and they passionately kissed. Then, they both smiled and started walking again.

CUT TO:

15. INT. BEACH - AFTERNOON

VIOLET and ESMERALDA walking along the beach together and holding hands. ESMERALDA then jumped on VIOLET's back and rode his back. They both laughed. VIOLET then put ESMERALDA down and they passionately kissed. Then, they both smiled and started walking again.

FLASH TO:

16. EXT. RESTAURANT INTO STREET - NIGHT

VIOLET and ESMERALDA leaving a restaurant in the city and walking back to ESMERALDA's apartment. Where they were walking along the city street that was lighted with stores and street lights. They both were smiling.

17. EXT. STREET-NIGHT

They were both walking along the shops and street lights. When all of a sudden it started to rain down hard upon them. They, then both looked at each other in annoyance. They were holding hands and started running. Evidently, the rain was so bad that they gave up. They just then started to walk and they started laughing.

VIOLET

Why?

ESMERALDA

Ugh! It's raining.

VIOLET

This sucks.

ESMERALDA

We are already wet.

VIOLET

Ugh.

ESMERALDA

Well. At least it isn't lightning.

VIOLET

(sarcastically) Oh, real nice.

ESMERALDA

Anyways. We are here at my condo. Together, they went into the condo.

18. INT. ESMERALDA'S CONDO - NIGHT

They entered the condo and took off their clothes down to their panties and bra. They passionately kissed as they went to make love in the bedroom. Darkness engulfed them.

CUT TO:

19. EXT. GARDEN - AFTERNOON

Together, they walked through the garden full of fountains, ponds, bushes, plants and flowers. They took under all the scenic view as they strolled through. Then, they found a table in the shade for a picnic. They sat down to eat and began eating.

ESMERALDA

It is a nice day outside.

VIOLET

Yes. It is.

ESMERALDA

You were an amazing lover in bed last night.

VIOLET

Thanks. You returned the favor as well.

ESMERALDA

I'm infatuated with you.

VIOLET

You are insatiable in bed. I can't keep my hands off of you.

ESMERALDA

Pleasure to be your pleasure.

VIOLET

It's at times like these when I'm in drought that I have always been thankful to have a vagina.

ESMERALDA

Nice.

VIOLET

That is very interesting.

ESMERALDA

You are absolutely stunning.

VIOLET

You are as well.

ESMERALDA

What is it that turns you on the most about me?

VIOLET

Your beautiful body and face. You are so hot. Your looks really do make my libido get aroused.

ESMERALDA

Your mind, words, and how you are romantic. You are good looking, but also have charm.

VIOLET

We are sitting in here and excuse me if I say so, but I can't stop thinking about how gorgeous you look naked.

ESMERALDA

Then, I will enjoy teasing you until tonight.

VIOLET

It's fine to tease, but only if you will give it up. Losing the clothes is always a positive.

ESMERALDA

I enjoy being naked around you. It's very enjoyable watching you drool over me and not be able to keep your hands off me.

VIOLET

My hands belong on you and with me exploring you.

ESMERALDA

You are a wonderland as I am a wonderland to you.

VIOLET smiled at ESMERALDA and rubbed her hand. They then continued back to eating and looking at each other.

VIOLET

Your heart is beautiful. I get lost in it.

ESMERALDA

Your heart is truly wonderful.

VIOLET

Where I do get lost in all of you.

ESMERALDA

You are to me what I am to you.

VIOLET

We truly do belong together.

ESMERALDA

We become taken deeper down under all of the love that we share together.

VIOLET

Our love is what makes us beautiful. You are beautiful to me. I fall more in love with you every day. You are the love of my life and my heart that churns from within mine for you.

ESMERALDA

You are my heart's desire. We belong together.

VIOLET

My heart wanders lonely without you. Why are we meant to long for things, if they aren't meant to be had? For whom does my heart long for?

ESMERALDA

Why you long for my heart. As my heart longs for yours. Our love was meant to lead us to each other. Our paths were paved towards each other.

VIOLET

My heart has led me to you and forever, since the day that I first met you I have been happy. My heart beats for you and your love. Your love has changed me in many ways. It makes me feel alive. It makes my emotions come to life.

ESMERALDA

Your love does all of the same to me. I find myself lost in your love. My vagina is literally stuck on your vagina now. I think you have broken it for use with others.

VIOLET

Well. That is good. That means you're doing something right.

ESMERALDA and VIOLET were looking at each other with an intense stare.

ESMERALDA

You know every day, I fall deeper in love with you. It is a constant.

VIOLET

That is good. Me too.

ESMERALDA

We were meant for each other.

VIOLET

We were meant to be together. We belong together.

ESMERALDA

I find that our time together is always fun. That we never run out of fun things to do or about things to talk about.

VIOLET

That is true. We always have something to talk about.

ESMERALDA

Time has gone past me. I have only learned to love you more and more.

VIOLET

Me as well.

ESMERALDA

You know. I still don't think my career has peaked yet. I have yet to write more.

VIOLET

I have yet to write more also.

ESMERALDA

I enjoy what I do.

VIOLET

So, do I.

ESMERALDA

I'm captivated by watching you work also.

VIOLET

Me too. You are interesting to watch work.

ESMERALDA

Charmed.

VIOLET

You make things quite interesting I would have to say.

ESMERALDA

Yes. There is never a dull moment with us.

VIOLET

There aren't many people that you can find and not get bored of or have nothing to talk about. You are one of those people.

ESMERALDA

That is us. Never a dull moment.

VIOLET

Esmeralda, you'll never break my heart, will you?

ESMERALDA

Not intentionally. I do think that we will always remain in love together.

VIOLET

I hope so. Sometimes, a breakup occurs for a one-sided relationship. When it is out of a two-sided relationship. Sometimes, the breakup is mutual and from both sides of the relationship. Where both fall out of love. Not one person falling out of love and the other still being in love.

ESMERALDA

That is so. This would be my first really true heartbreak.

VIOLET

I've had my heartbroken already.

ESMERALDA

That is very painful. I am sorry to hear that. I can say that I am glad though, because I have you now.

VIOLET

I'm glad also. I found you. I learned what love is and isn't. I learned what falling in love is and what falling out of love is. I learned what I thought was love, but wasn't. All of it led me to you, Esmeralda.

ESMERALDA

That is so true. Everything leads us to each other. We were meant to be together. We are a beautiful couple.

VIOLET

That's who we are. We are a beautiful couple. We also compliment each other very well.

ESMERALDA

That we do.

VIOLET

It is so nice out. I'm finished. Let's get going. We have to get ready to go out tomorrow night. I have to get some of my poetry novel written.

ESMERALDA

I have to get some of my opera written as well. Brilliance in the masterpiece that is in the making.

They stood up and throw out their trash in the garbage CAN next to them. They, then started walking out of the GARDEN. Where they went past roses, flowers, bushes, ponds, and other plants.

DISSOLVE TO:

20. EXT. WALKWAY ALONG THE RIVER - NIGHT

They were holding hands as they walked along down the river. They saw many boats passing them by. Everything was very well lit. They were strolling past other people and weren't really paying attention to the people as they were engrossed in each other. The lights lit up their way as well as all of the buildings. The full moon also lit their path as they walked. They held hands and longingly looked into each other's eyes. They, then stared at each other.

VIOLET
I'm enchanted to be with you.

ESMERALDA
As am I to be with you.

VIOLET
We belong together.

ESMERALDA
Everything is great about you. You make me passionate about all of the wonders of your love.

VIOLET
I want to stand with you on an island in the ocean naked and hold your beautiful body under the full moonlight.

ESMERALDA
What if there are people there?

VIOLET
We will go to a secluded place.

ESMERALDA
Well, if there are no people. Then, that is fine with me.

VIOLET

Then, we'll put that on our to-do list.

ESMERALDA

We have a to-do list?

VIOLET

Yes. I made us a to-do list. Things that we should do when we are together to make it special.

ESMERALDA

Aww. How cute.

VIOLET

I try.

They both smiled as they walked past people and down the walkway. Where they also saw boats passing them by.

ESMERALDA

It's so beautiful out here tonight. I am truly mesmerized with all of your passionate love for me. We make such a great and beautiful couple.

VIOLET

We absolutely belong together. We are amazing. Our love is a fantasy that has come true.

ESMERALDA

I am so glad that I was noisy and noticed you. That I went over to meet you.

VIOLET

Yes or perhaps we wouldn't be in a relationship together. That is so.

ESMERALDA

We have the perfect relationship.

VIOLET

Yes. We fight. Then, we always makeup. That's just what we do. Nothing that has caused our relationship to end yet though.

ESMERALDA

If it rains. It's wet t-shirt time.

VIOLET

Nice. I'm trying to have a serious conversation and you are talking about us having a wet t-shirt time.

ESMERALDA

That is so very true.

VIOLET

You know that is funny though. You do have a good sense of humor.

ESMERALDA

Yes. We both have a great sense of humor. As well as we get each other's sense of humor. So, that makes us get along great.

VIOLET

That is so. Our humor suits us both.

ESMERALDA

You are the passion to my heart. My hearts loving desire.

VIOLET

The heart from within my heart of passion that I have for you.

ESMERALDA

That is so.

VIOLET

You are almost too much.

ESMERALDA

You really are.

VIOLET

You are so beautiful. They were in front of the restaurant that they would be going into.

They stopped and VIOLET wrapped her arms around ESMERALDA and pulled ESMERALDA into her. ESMERALDA held VIOLET. VIOLET leaned in and kissed ESMERALDA. ESMERALDA then giggled as they walked into the restaurant.

DISSOLVE TO:

21. INT. LIGHTHOUSE- NIGHT

VIOLET and ESMERALDA were sitting down at the table at the restaurant outside on the porch that was overlooking the street. Their meal had come and they begin to eat. Cars where driving past them and people were walking by. There was a full moon out and it was nice out.

ESMERALDA
You picked a nice place.

VIOLET
It is an easy night out.

ESMERALDA
There is quite a busy scene that I would say.

VIOLET
So, I thought I would just tell you that I am falling more and more in love with you.

ESMERALDA
I am taken with our romance. You have swept me away in your love.

VIOLET
(whispers) My passion lays with your heart and if I might add between your legs.

ESMERALDA
We are in public. That is naughty of you.

VIOLET

You love it. You know it.

ESMERALDA

That is so. You are witty and clever with your humor. It is part of why I love you.

VIOLET

And part of why I love you is why my heart longs for yours.

ESMERALDA

As your heart is beautiful.

VIOLET

So, great being a couple. We must never breakup.

ESMERALDA

Yes. No breakups. Only lots of love.

VIOLET

Till our hearts content.

ESMERALDA

Well. My heart is never content. I am greedy.

VIOLET

That you are. I am greedy and want to steal all of your kisses away.

ESMERALDA

That is so very true.

VIOLET

We are smitten together with each other's hearts of passion.

ESMERALDA

Is that so?

VIOLET

That is so.

ESMERALDA

Our love is beauty. Our beauty is love.

VIOLET

You know that it is beautiful outside. We have a great view of the full moon and the ocean.

ESMERALDA

Anyhow. Our future together is going to be great.

VIOLET

We belong to each other.

ESMERALDA

Our hearts are great together. We are beauty.

VIOLET

(smiles).

They ate. They longingly looked at each other.

VIOLET (CONT'D)

We only grow closer together with time.

ESMERALDA

I know.

VIOLET

I never get tired of you.

ESMERALDA

There is never a dull moment with us. That is so.

VIOLET

You know that you love my charm. I am charming.

ESMERALDA

I do. Don't push it.

VIOLET

So, touching. This is your love machine though, darling.

ESMERALDA

I know. Sweetie. You are everything to me,

VIOLET

We get lost in our love for each other.

ESMERALDA

You know that our hearts belong to each other as we get lost together from within each other.

VIOLET

You are everything to me.

ESMERALDA

Everything blossoms in the hearts of ours.

VIOLET

You know that our future looks great together. We are each other's everything.

ESMERALDA

You are so awful when you don't get what you want. You throw tantrums.

VIOLET

So, learn to embrace my tantrums. My tantrums are justified.

ESMERALDA

You need to just overcome that.

VIOLET

Whatever.

ESMERALDA

Our future is looking good. We are moving in together.

VIOLET

Yes. Technically, we already live together though. As we are staying at each other's places.

ESMERALDA

Like two vacation homes that we both live in.

VIOLET

Yes.

ESMERALDA

I've only ever loved you. I have never stopped loving you.

VIOLET

I have only grown to love you more and more.

ESMERALDA

I have only grown to love you more and more as well.

VIOLET

Everything about our love is enchanting.

ESMERALDA

There is never a dull moment with us.

VIOLET

That is so very true.

ESMERALDA

We are never bored. We are always doing something fun or laughing together.

VIOLET

Life is about the amount of laughs we take that puts a smile on our face.

ESMERALDA

Well put.

VIOLET

I'm smitten with all of your love that you give me.

ESMERALDA

As I am to you.

VIOLET

You seduce me.

ESMERALDA

You seduced me with your words.

VIOLET

I give pleasure to your ears.

ESMERALDA

Yes, you do.

VIOLET

That's not all that I give pleasure to. Remember, I give pleasure to your body as well.

ESMERALDA

My body demands your pleasure.

VIOLET

I am more than happy to oblige.

ESMERALDA

Time is telling of our beautiful love.

VIOLET

You speak of our love very beautifully.

ESMERALDA

That is because our love is very beautiful.

VIOLET

That it is.

ESMERALDA

It is as beautiful as a flower in bloom.

VIOLET

Beauty is of our love.

ESMERALDA

Our love is beauty.

VIOLET

I'm taken with you.

ESMERALDA

You have a way with words sweetie.

VIOLET

We will be together forever.

ESMERALDA

Our souls are now intertwined.

VIOLET

Our souls are beautiful.

ESMERALDA

That is so.

VIOLET

Love is a wonder that is beautiful.

ESMERALDA

Our love is something that we do explore along together.

VIOLET

That is so very true.

ESMERALDA

I get lost in your passion for me sometimes. It sweeps me away into your world.

VIOLET

I like sharing my world with you.

ESMERALDA

Me too.

VIOLET

I like making all of your dreams that you have come true.

ESMERALDA

Aw. How sweet. That is beautiful.

VIOLET

It is. It is beautiful like you.

ESMERALDA

You are so sweet to me.

VIOLET

Passion befalls our great love.

ESMERALDA

We have a passion that burns so strong for each other.

VIOLET

Our dreams are all coming true with each other.

ESMERALDA

That is so. Dreams that are had are meant to come true.

VIOLET

You are my dream come true.

ESMERALDA

You are my dream as well.

VIOLET

We belong together.

ESMERALDA

As we have fallen in love together.

VIOLET

Never has anything been said that has been more true.

ESMERALDA

I have always loved you. Since we first talked. I knew that we would be together forever.

VIOLET

I did as well.

ESMERALDA

You are a beautiful lover.

VIOLET

You are my beautiful lover.

ESMERALDA

Forever our love will soar to the greatest heights.

VIOLET

With no limits.

ESMERALDA

I have always longed for a love such as our love.

VIOLET

Well it has come true.

ESMERALDA

I know. I am very pleased.

VIOLET

Well. You deserved it.

ESMERALDA

Very pleased.

VIOLET

I am pleased with you.

ESMERALDA

I am pleased with us.

VIOLET

I love you.

ESMERALDA

I love you too.

VIOLET

We fit in perfectly together.

ESMERALDA

That we do. That we do.

VIOLET

So beautiful.

ESMERALDA

You are such a romantic.

VIOLET

I am. It makes everything more interesting. Dinner was delicious. I'm finished.

ESMERALDA

I am too. This was a great date.

VIOLET

Let's go sweetie. They finished dinner. They, then got up and left and disappeared out the door.

DISSOLVE TO:

22. INT. VIOLET'S PENTHOUSE - AFTERNOON

The moving van pulls away. VIOLET and ESMERALDA have finished unpacking all of ESMERALDA's boxes. VIOLET then threw out all of the boxes into one of the empty closet. She then came back into the master bedroom to ESMERALDA.

ESMERALDA
Almost all finished unpacking my stuff.

VIOLET
That's good.

ESMERALDA
I just think that this is the best move for us.

VIOLET
Oh. You do?

ESMERALDA
Yes. I mean we have already been staying at each other's place for a while now. It's like we already live together.

VIOLET
I am glad that you are moving in with me. It is a big step for us.

ESMERALDA
I would agree. I am excited.

VIOLET
Now, we will be around each other more.

ESMERALDA
That is true. Yet, we already are around each other a lot.

VIOLET
Yes. We are, but that is because we love each other very much.

VIOLET walked up behind ESMERALDA and wrapped her arms around ESMERALDA. ESMERALDA turned her head and VIOLET kissed her.

VIOLET (CONT'D)
You are so sexy.

ESMERALDA

Some is feeling frisky.

VIOLET

You have no idea.

ESMERALDA

I do.

VIOLET

Living together is going to be a lot of fun.

ESMERALDA

I am glad we are taking the next step to our relationship by moving in.

VIOLET

We will be together forever.

ESMERALDA

Yes. We will.

VIOLET

Together, forever and always.

ESMERALDA

Hold me and tell me you love me.

VIOLET

I love you.

ESMERALDA

I love you too.

VIOLET

Come on sweetie.

VIOLET and ESMERALDA then striped down to their lingerie and kissed as they climbed under the covers in bed. They passionately kissed under the covers as they played.

ESMERALDA

You kiss beautifully.

VIOLET

You are a good kisser also.

ESMERALDA

I'm just glad you're not slobbering on me.

VIOLET

Very funny.

ESMERALDA

Someone is feeling frisky.

VIOLET

I couldn't help myself. You just looked so sexy and seduced me with your body.

ESMERALDA

My pleasure.

VIOLET

Your lips are my pleasure. Your lips are so soft and supple.

VIOLET kissed her again and then pulled back.

ESMERALDA

I get lost in your kiss. Kiss me again.

VIOLET kissed her again. VIOLET then looked at her cleavage.

VIOLET

Your cleavage is so beautiful. My eyes are pleased for they see beauty.

ESMERALDA

Kiss my cleavage.

VIOLET gently kissed ESMERALDA's cleavage and then her lips again. The passion was stirring.

VIOLET

We will always be together.

ESMERALDA

Why? Because we make love that gives us lots of pleasure.

VIOLET

Yes. Also, that we love each other.

ESMERALDA

Your heart never ceases to amaze me.

VIOLET

Your heart amazes mine.

VIOLET placed her hand on ESMERALDA's heart.

VIOLET (CONT'D)

Because I can feel your heart.

ESMERALDA

I love you.

VIOLET

I love you too.

VIOLET removed her hand. They passionately kissed.

CUT TO:

23. INT. PENTHOUSE OFFICE - NIGHT

VIOLET is in her office at her desk and is writing her poetry novel at a computer. ESMERALDA is at her desk and is writing her opera.

FADE OUT: CLOSING TITLE: (V.O.)

ESMERALDA and VIOLET were a beautiful couple. They didn't agree on everything, but did with a lot of things. They were beautiful lovers who got lost in their world of romance. Where everything around them disappeared. ESMERALDA went on to write five more operas. VIOLET went on to write ten more poetry novels. Their journey through their love started out beautiful and had no ending. For their love was a love full of passion and romance. Their love was of great wonder. An epic tale of love remained unraveling itself beautifully amongst the lovers. Where they got to know each other better than themselves. Where the time passed and they learned more about each other. Their romance was forever shining. The beauty in their love was enchanting. Forever they would remain in love. Forever a tale of their love would unravel. For they were the fairest of lovers. Beauty was their love. A love that told a story of passion. A romance filled with wonder. These beautiful lover's hearts of passion swept them away and they got lost in all of each other's passionate love. Where beautiful lovers came together in beauty. Where masterpieces were written. The wonders of their love beautifully unfolded before the lovers. They went on a journey through their love for each other. True love leaving them enchanted. Everything about their love was beautiful. Forever they were intertwined from within a grand love of epic proportions. Beauty was their everything. Everything was their love. Their life was their love towards each other. Love was beauty. They were beauty. Where a tale of a true love would forever play itself out. An enchanting love unveiled itself. Forever the beautiful lovers danced in an endless romance.

FADE OUT:

THE END

Author's Biography

Courtney Asunmaa enjoys writing romantic novels, adventures, or comedies. Born in 1985, writing has been one of her passions. She enjoys traveling. She earned an Undergraduate Certificate in Paralegal Studies in 2010 at Ashworth College. She earned a Bachelor of Arts in Finance at Ashford University in 2015. She earned her Masters of Accountancy at Ashford University in 2017. She is currently getting her Doctor of Business Administration in Finance at Walden University. Courtney also writes opera librettos, plays, song lyrics, TV scripts, movie screenplays, novels, and poems.

www.ingramcontent.com/pod-product-compliance
Lightning Source LLC
Chambersburg PA
CBHW021655120626
46545CB00002B/867